AF231005

ROYAL RECORDERS

BOOK ONE

1

Royal Recorders

Levels 1-7

Royal Recorders © 2022 Donna Rhodenizer / Red Castle Publishing

By Donna Rhodenizer

www.royalrecorders.com

Copyright © 2022 Donna Rhodenizer/Red Castle Publishing

COPYRIGHT INFORMATION

All rights to reproduce the material covered in this copyright in any form or by any means of reproduction are reserved by the publisher. Copies of material covered in this copyright may not be prepared for resale or distributed to any other individual to make copies.

Printed student books may not be copied unless a digital Royal Recorders program and copying license have been purchased.

Accompaniment tracks may be used by a teacher with students in a single school/teaching assignment (multiple schools – one teacher), private teaching studio or homeschool. Accompaniment tracks shall not be copied, reproduced and/or distributed to other individuals who should purchase their own copy.

Copyright - Short and sweet (without legal jargon)

If you are interested in doing the right thing, the legal thing, and supporting teaching colleagues like me who are creating teaching resources, here's what you can do.

Printed books
- If you want printed student books, please purchase them, DON'T photocopy them.
- If you want to print your own copies of student books, please purchase a copy license.

Accompaniment tracks
- Accompaniment tracks are a great motivational tool for students when practicing. Whatever you need or want to do to create access to the accompaniment tracks for your students is fine by us (Donna Rhodenizer/Andy Duinker/Red Castle Publishing). Accompaniments may be shared using Google Classroom and similar platforms used in educational settings.
- **Please do not** purchase tracks and copy them to give to another teacher. The program cost is as reasonable as possible so each school should purchase their own legal copy.

Royal Recorders, created by Donna Rhodenizer
Contributing Editor, Andy Duinker

The complete Royal Recorders program includes:
Student Book 1 (2nd Edition) ISBN 978-1-989720-14-1
Student Book 2 (2nd Edition) ISBN 978-1-989720-15-8
Teacher Guide (2nd Edition) ISBN 978-1-989720-16-5
(Books have print and digital download options)
Accompaniment Tracks – Book 1
Accompaniment Tracks – Book 2
Instructional Videos

Copyright © 2022 Donna Rhodenizer / Red Castle Publishing

www.royalrecorders.com

Red Castle Publishing
20 Silver Fox Ave., PO Box 10001
New Minas, NS CANADA
B4N 5K1

Welcome to *Royal Recorders*

I am so excited to be part of your musical development as you learn to play recorder. I got my first recorder when I was eight years old. My mom used to encourage me to go outside to practice. The cows on my family farm would stand around and listen to me practice and eventually I improved enough that I could play in the house! I will warn you that a lot of people think recorders are loud and ugly instruments. I am here to tell you that recorders can be used to play fun music, exciting songs and beautiful tunes. Of course, getting started there will be some squawks and squeaks. With a little bit of time and some practice, be prepared to amaze your family and friends and also have a lot of fun making music along the way.

There are 22 songs in **Book 1**. The first recorder tunes I wrote for you have only 2 notes. When you play them with the Royal Recorder accompaniment tracks, even these simple songs are fun to play and sound pretty good. As you learn to play each group of songs, you will be awarded new Knight levels. It is exciting to keep improving and being awarded new knight levels as you master each new group of song challenges.

You will have the chance to write your own songs along the way. Take what you know and turn it into your very own song! Share your music with a friend or your family. Get them involved by getting them to play along, even if it is tapping the beat as you play.

Take some time to practice naming notes using the Knightly note-naming worksheets. Even just 2 minutes a day can make a difference in being able to recognize notes quickly. Knowing the note names will help you when you are working on new song challenges.

As you learn more notes, the songs become even more interesting. I have chosen some of my favourite beautiful melodies, fun dance tunes, a few melodies you may recognize as sing-along songs, and I have also written many new songs for you to enjoy. When you are able to play interesting songs with a good tone, play your recorder for family and friends, your grandparents, and at community events. I hope they will realize that the recorder can be a fun instrument that can provide music enjoyment for everyone.

Once you have mastered all the songs in Book 1, you will find 23 more songs waiting for you in **Book 2**. There are also extra songs available at www.royalrecorders.com. You will not run out of songs to play! At the end of Book 2 you will be a Gold Knight and you will have developed amazing recorder skills.

When it is time to play recorders with my students, they are excited and I am excited. We have lots of fun making music and I know you can have a great time making music with your recorder as well. I am so happy to invite you to enter the Royal Recorders kingdom. Get ready to make beautiful music with your recorder!

Good luck with your Royal Recorders song challenges. See you at the castle!

Donna

ROYAL RECORDERS

Prepare for your Quest!

How to hold your recorder

- Left hand is at the top the recorder. Always!
  - ➢ Left thumb is used to cover the thumb-hole on the back.
  - ➢ Left hand index, middle and ring fingers cover the first three holes.
  - ➢ Left hand little finger has nothing to do – it can just "hang out" and rest!
- Right hand is at the bottom of the recorder.
  - ➢ Right hand fingers are used to cover the bottom four holes
  - ➢ Right thumb provides support on the back of the recorder (between holes 4 and 5).
- Keep the recorder tilting down at a bit of an angle (not straight out like a trumpet).
- Elbows are down, relaxed and fairly close to the body.

Fingers

- Use the flat pads of your fingers (not the tips) to cover the holes.
- Cover the holes completely or air will escape, creating squeaks or an incorrect note.
- When adjusting and correcting your fingers, try to feel the holes under your fingers. Don't remove your recorder to look at your fingers. That changes the angle of your hands and as soon as you return the recorder to your mouth, the fingers will move and create the same issue again.

Mouth position

- The mouthpiece of the recorder is placed on the bottom lip with only the tip of the mouthpiece in your mouth.
- Your upper lip will press down gently, like saying the sound "mmm".
- The mouthpiece should not be touching your teeth when you play.

Breathing

- Use gentle breath when playing. This should feel like the breath you make when you clean your glasses or trying to create fog on a window.
- Practice whispering "du du du" and notice where your tongue is touching (the roof of your mouth behind your front teeth). You will use your tongue in this same spot to stop and start notes. Be careful not to push the air too forcefully or you will get squeaks.

Stop squeaks!

- Squeaks happen when you blow too hard, finger holes are not completely covered, or the angle of the recorder is out too straight.

Rest position

- When it is not being played, the recorder should be placed in rest position across your lap. Rest position is used when the teacher is giving instructions, before class has begun or any time you are waiting and should NOT be playing.

Royal Recorders Copyright © 2022 Donna Rhodenizer / Red Castle Publishing
www.royalrecorders.com

Some practice advice

- Do finger push-ups every day:
  - ✓ Without blowing any air, use your left hand fingers to cover the first three holes on the front of the recorder.
  - ✓ Lift the ring finger up and put it back down several times.
  - ✓ Do the same thing with other finger combinations, lifting and replacing the fingers to strengthen the finger muscles.
- Practice slowly.
- Play the difficult sections of each song first and then play the whole song. If you always stop when you make a mistake and re-start at the beginning, the parts you really need to work on get less practice and only the beginning of the song improves.
- If the song is not supposed to go fast, don't play it fast!

Reference section – Music Symbols and Theory

Music is written on a **staff** with five lines and four spaces. When counting lines and spaces, start at the bottom and count up. Like a ladder, the higher you climb, the higher the sounds will be.

A sign called a **treble clef** is located at the beginning of the staff. A staff with a treble clef will have notes that are high sounds.

Music is divided into groups of beats. These are called **measures** or **bars**. The groups of beats are divided by using **bar lines**. A small number at the beginning of each line will indicate the **bar number** at that point. A **double bar line** will indicate the end of the song.

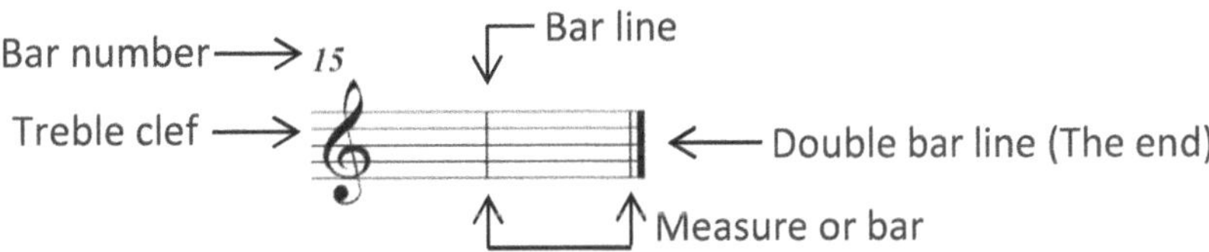

Each note on the lines and spaces of the staff has its own name. Short lines are added for notes that are written above and below the staff. The short lines are called ledger lines.

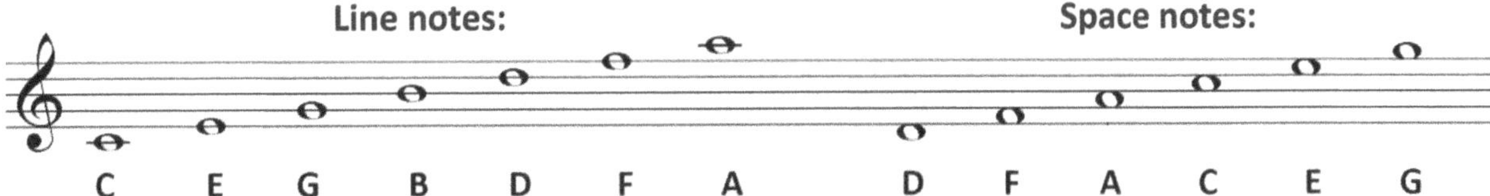

Time signature
The top number of a time signature tells you how many beats are in each bar.
The bottom number tells you what kind of note gets one beat.

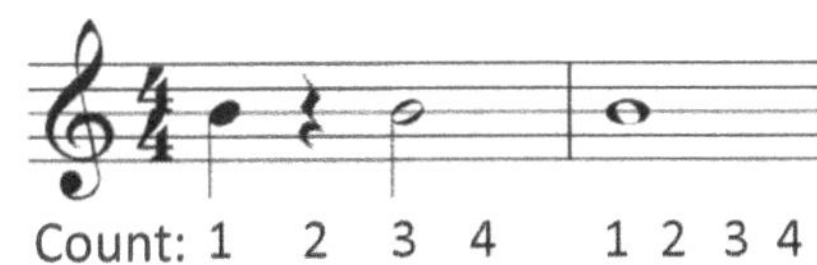

Note Value *Knight's Helmet*

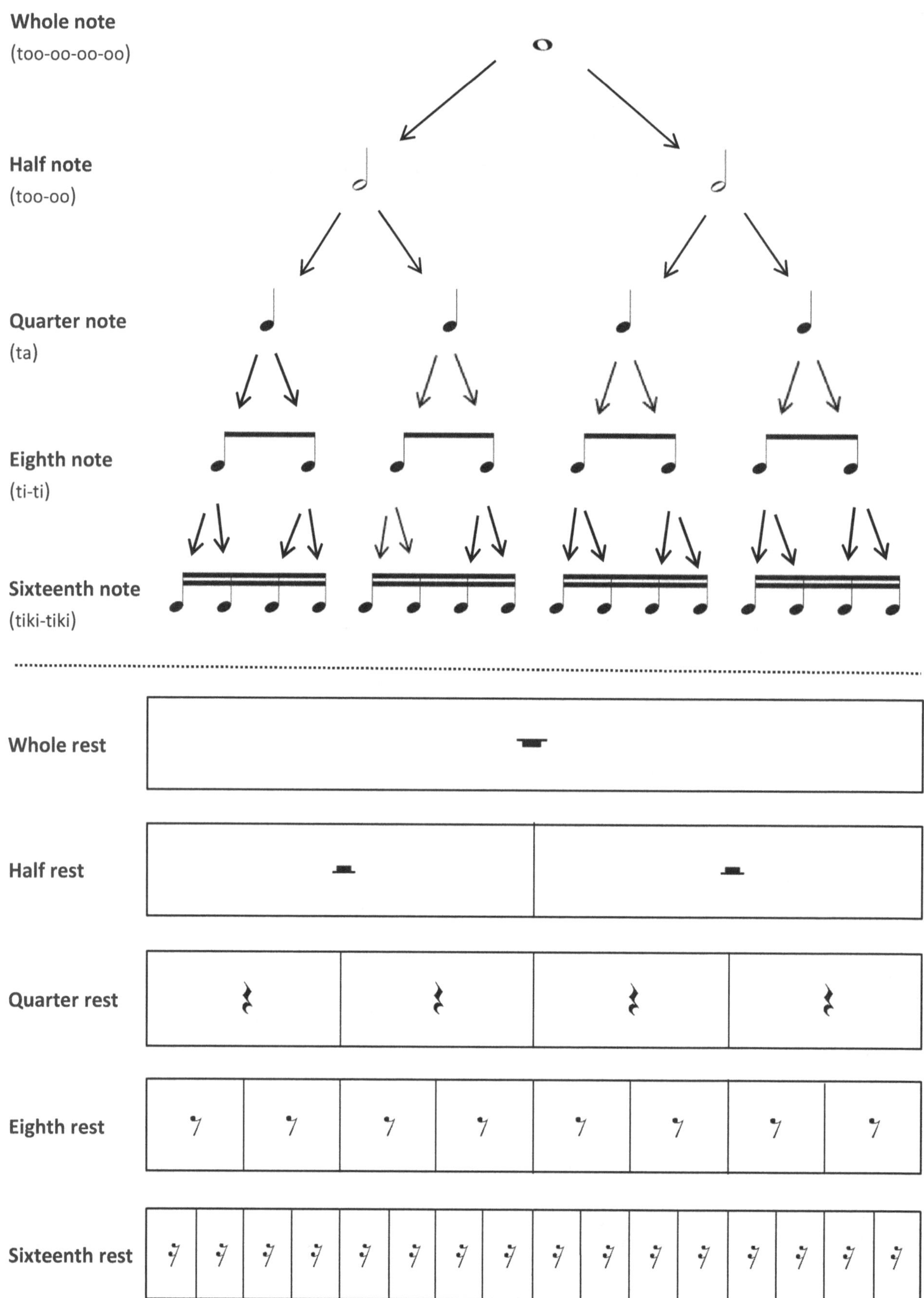

Knightly Note-naming Challenges (pages 23-35)

Each Knight level has note-naming challenges at the back of your book (Sheets start on p.24,
following a page of instructions on p.23).

Being able to recognize and name the notes will help you as you learn new songs.

Royal Recorder Knights can practice naming notes with 30-note and 60-note challenges.

How many notes can you name in two minutes?

How long does it take you to name all 30 notes?

How long does it take you to name all 60 notes?

Try to improve your accuracy and your speed.

Note-naming sheets are available at **www.royalrecorders.com**

Video Testing Instructions

At the beginning of each testing video you create for your Royal Recorders Song Challenges,
please say:

- your name
- the class you are in
- the song challenge you are playing
- the Knight level

Example:

My name is **Donna**.

I am in **Ms. King's grade 5 class**.

I am playing ***Jolly Minstrels*** for my **Turquoise Knight Song Challenge**.

Accompaniment Tracks

Downloadable accompaniment tracks are available for all songs in this book.

There are two accompaniment tracks for each song:

- practice speed
- performance speed

Accompaniments are in a variety of fun styles to help your
Royal Recorders Song Challenges sound GREAT!

Ask your teacher about accompaniment tracks or go to:

www.royalrecorders.com

Royal Recorders Copyright © 2022 Donna Rhodenizer / Red Castle Publishing
www.royalrecorders.com

WHITE, YELLOW, ORANGE
Knights in Training

First three notes:

G	A	B

Left hand   **Left hand**   **Left hand**

Go to pages 24-27 for your White, Yellow and Orange Knight note-naming challenges.

Royal Recorders Copyright © 2022 Donna Rhodenizer / Red Castle Publishing
www.royalrecorders.com

WHITE, YELLOW, ORANGE
Knights in Training

Repeat sign

There is a repeat sign shown at the end of bar 4 in the sample below. This sign means that you will go back and repeat from the beginning of the song. (Sample from Yellow Knight song *Big Bad G, p.9*)

You will find this type of repeat sign in each of the White and Yellow Knight song challenges (pages 8 and 9) and in the Orange Knight songs *Up and Down* and *B A G of Surprises* (p. 10).

Repeat sign (a different kind!)

Flamenco Flair has two different kinds of repeat signs. (Yellow Knight Song Challenge p.9)

At the end of bar 8, the repeat sign will send you back to the beginning of the song. We already know about this kind of repeat sign. You will return to bar 1 and repeat the first eight bars.

But there is **another repeat sign** at the end of bar 16. This repeat sign is one of a matched pair. The repeat sign at the end of bar 16 will send you to find its matching sign at the beginning of bar 9 to show you the section to be repeated.

Time signature

The top number of the time signature for *Flamenco Flair* shows that there are 3 beats in every bar. The 4 on the bottom means a quarter note is worth one beat. The half note (worth two beats) is given another beat because of the dot, and will be held for the whole bar (3 beats).

Tonguing

The quick notes in *Flamenco Flair* will be easier to play if tonguing is used. Tonguing is when you start and stop the air flow by putting your tongue on the roof of your mouth behind the top teeth. It is like whispering "du" as each note is played. Be careful not to push the air too hard or you will get squeaks.

1 - WHITE KNIGHT Song Challenges

G and A All Day

Donna Rhodenizer

He B G Bees

Donna Rhodenizer

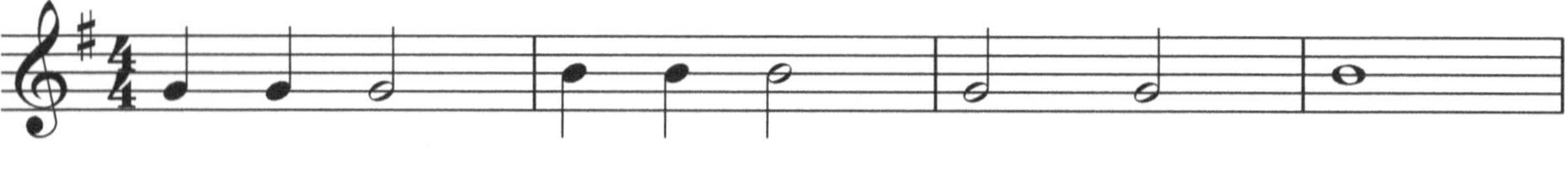

Baa, Baa, Baa

Donna Rhodenizer

Royal Recorders Copyright © 2022 Donna Rhodenizer / Red Castle Publishing
www.royalrecorders.com

One, Two, Skip a Few

Donna Rhodenizer

Big Bad G

Donna Rhodenizer

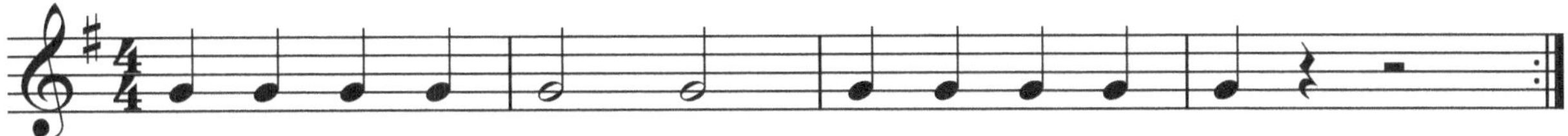

Flamenco Flair

Donna Rhodenizer

3 - ORANGE KNIGHT Song Challenges

Up and Down

Donna Rhodenizer

BAG of Surprises

Donna Rhodenizer

Fais dodo

French Folk Song

My G-A-B Composition

Compose your song using notes (G A B):   Composer_______________________

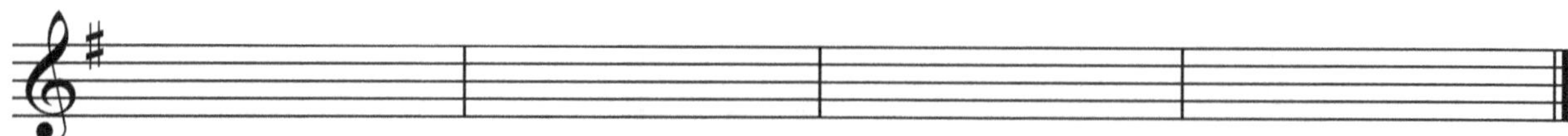

Compose using letter names for each note (G A B):

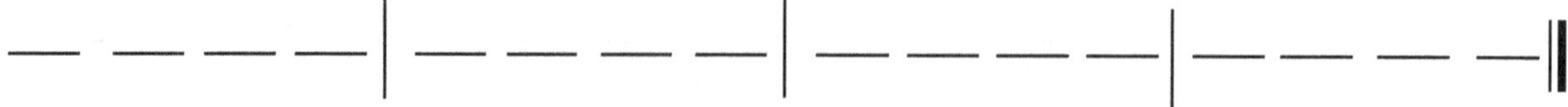

Royal Recorders Copyright © 2022 Donna Rhodenizer / Red Castle Publishing
www.royalrecorders.com

New note: Low E

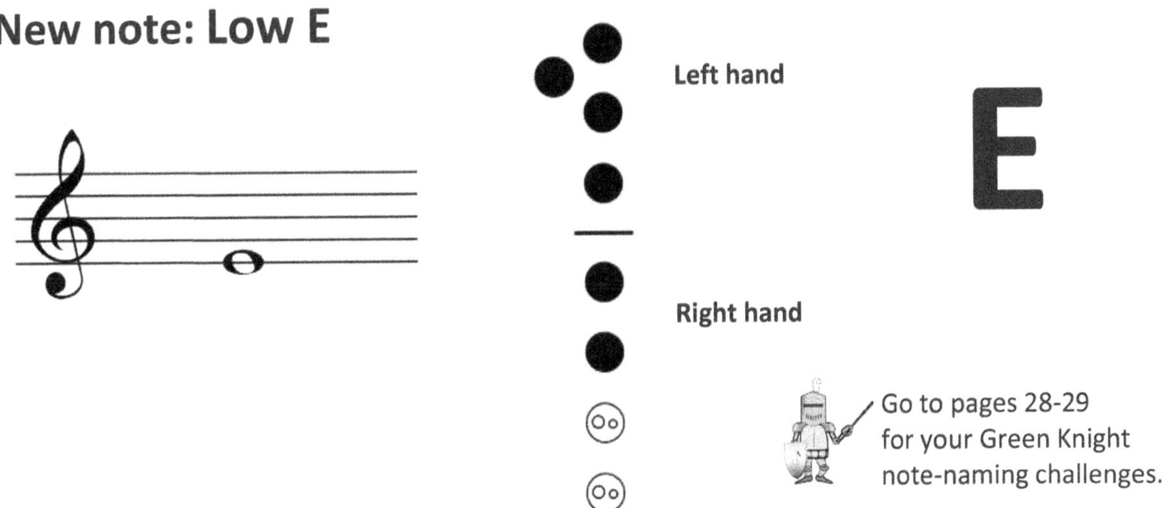

1st and 2nd ending

Sometimes when there is a repeat in the music, 1st and 2nd endings are used. Look at the sample below. You will play from the beginning of the song to the repeat at the end of the 1st ending (under the bracket with the 1. in it). Return to the beginning and play the section again. The second time you get to the bars in the 1st ending, skip over them and play the bars in the 2nd ending (under the bracket with the 2. in it) and continue to the end of the song. *Over Easy* has 1st and 2nd endings (p.12).

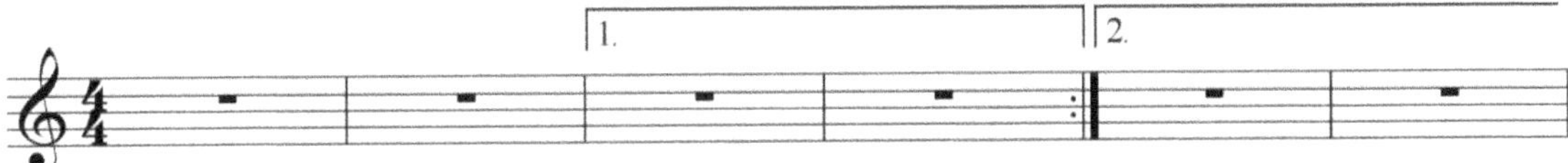

Phrase

A long curved line over multiple notes shows a phrase (a complete musical idea). These notes should be connected smoothly to each other. *Skin and Bones* includes the following phrase:

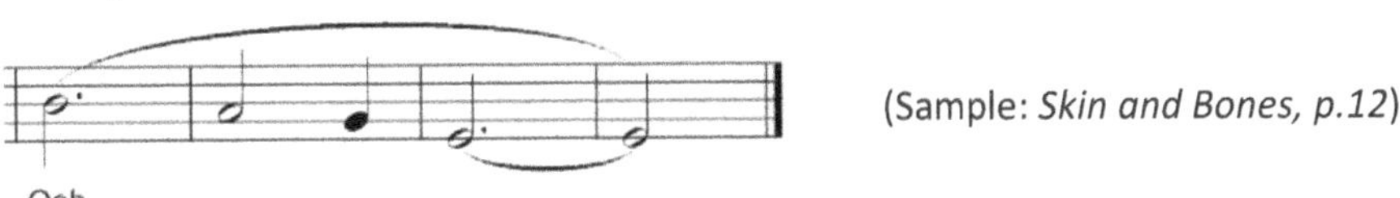

(Sample: *Skin and Bones*, p.12)

Tie

A line connecting two notes that are the same sound is a tie. This means that the value of both notes are added together. In the sample above (*Skin and Bones*, bar 7) the E that you play in bar 7 is held for a total of 5 beats (3+2).

There is also a tie in *Blues-E* (p.12). An accent is created when the note starts between beat one and beat two. This is called syncopation and it is often found in jazz and blues music.

(Sample: *Blues-E*)

Anacrusis

An anacrusis (or pickup beat) appears in a partial bar of music before bar 1. The beats used to create the anacrusis are "borrowed" from the last bar of the song. Together, they add up to the right number of beats for that time signature. *Skin and Bones* has an anacrusis (p.12).

Royal Recorders Copyright © 2022 Donna Rhodenizer / Red Castle Publishing
www.royalrecorders.com

4 - GREEN KNIGHT Song Challenges

Over Easy

Donna Rhodenizer

Royal Recorders Copyright © 2022 Donna Rhodenizer / Red Castle Publishing
www.royalrecorders.com

New note: **Low D**

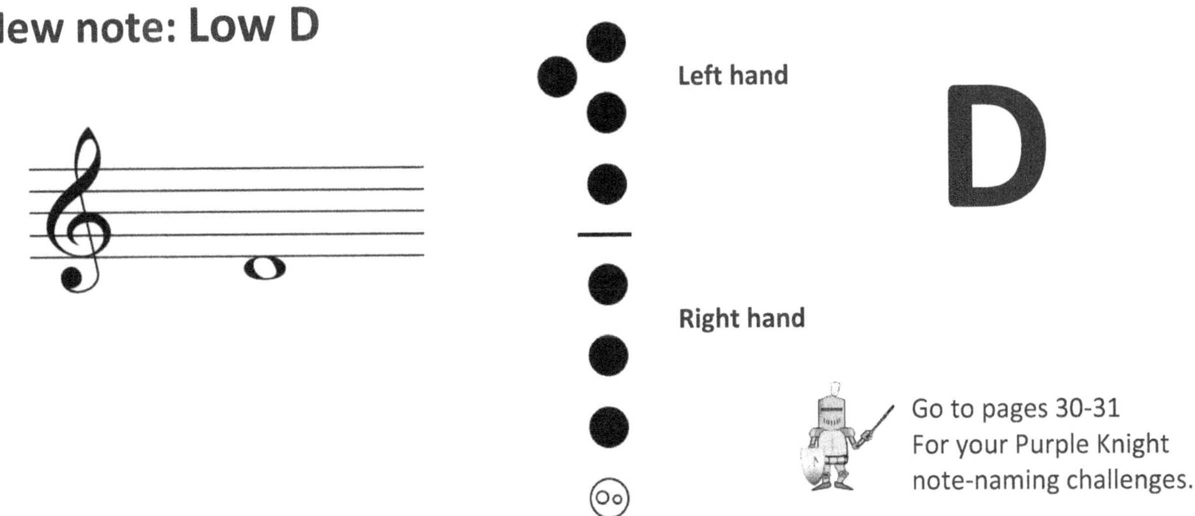

Go to pages 30-31 For your Purple Knight note-naming challenges.

Anacrusis

In the song *There's a Hole in My Bucket,* the 3/4 time signature shows that there will be 3 beats in every bar. However, before bar 1 there are two eighth notes that add up to only one beat, creating a partial bar. This is called an **anacrusis** or **pickup beat**. That beat has been "borrowed" from the last bar of the song (which only has 2 beats in it).

(Sample: *There's a Hole in My Bucket, p.14*)

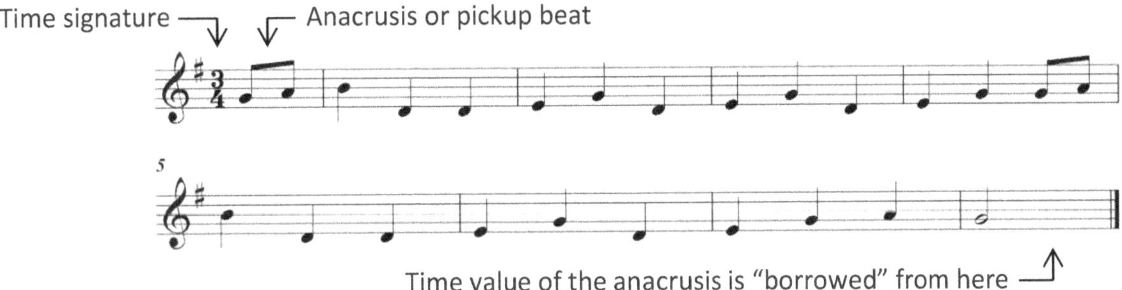

Swing the eighths

At the beginning of a song you may see the instruction: swing the eighths. This means that although it is written the same as two evenly spaced eighth (ti-ti) notes, you will hold the first one a little longer and shorten the second one. This will create a swinging or galloping feeling.

(Sample: *There's a Hole in My Bucket*)

Rhythm to practice

Old MacDonald (p.14) has tricky rhythms in bars 9-12. The words will be familiar: "*With a quack quack here and a quack quack there. Here a quack, there a quack, everywhere a quack quack.*" Thinking the words as you play may help you as you play the rhythm. Use tonguing (see explanation on p.7) for more help with the quick, quacky notes, but be careful - no squeaking!!!

Royal Recorders Copyright © 2022 Donna Rhodenizer / Red Castle Publishing
www.royalrecorders.com

5 - *PURPLE KNIGHT* Song Challenges

Go for a Stroll

Old MacDonald

There's a Hole in My Bucket

5 - PURPLE KNIGHT Song Challenges
COMPOSITION

Create your own 8-bar song: Use D E G A and B

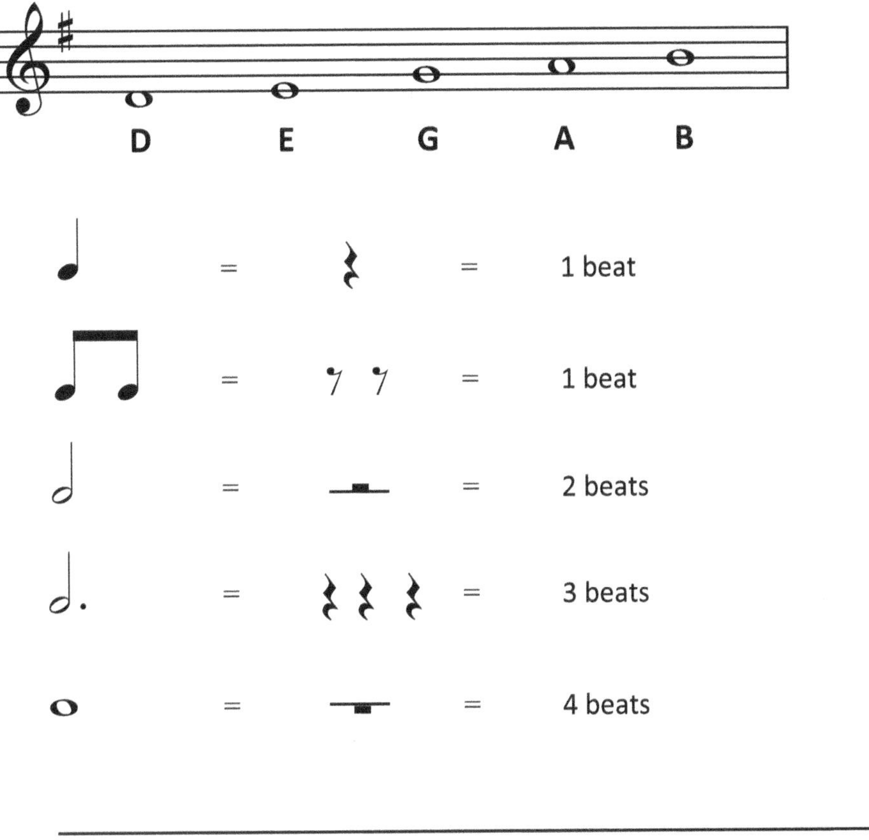

____
Title

Add **3** or **4** on top to create your time signature (beat groupings)

____
Composer

4

7

Copyright © ______   ____________________
Year   *Composer*

Royal Recorders Copyright © 2022 Donna Rhodenizer / Red Castle Publishing
www.royalrecorders.com

6 - *TURQUOISE KNIGHT* in Training

New note: High D (D')

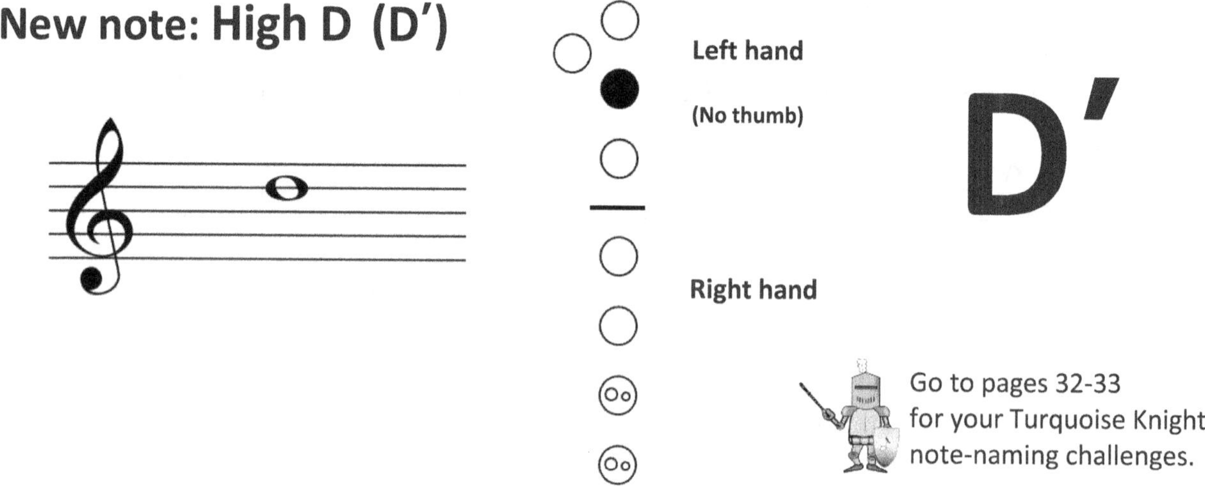

No thumb

This is the first recorder note you have learned that requires the thumb-hole to be left open (or uncovered). Because of its high pitch, high D must be played carefully so it does not create a harsh tone.

2/2 time signature

The time signature for *Lady of the Red Castle* (p.18) may look unfamiliar to you.
2/2 time means there are two beats in every bar and each half note is counted as one beat.

Rhythm element

The rhythm combination of an eighth note and two sixteenth notes is written in bar 5 (beat 3) of *À la claire fontaine* (p.18).

(sample of bar 5):

The rhythm indicated by arrows above has the same time value as two eighth notes. The eighth note and two sixteenth note combination also occurs in bar 6. The rhythm is read as ti tiki when using rhythm duration syllables (the first half of the beat is a ti and the other half is a tiki).
It may be helpful to review the **Note Value Knight's Helmet** on page 4.

Slur

In bars 5 and 6 of the song *À la claire fontaine* (p.18) you will see a curved line, called a slur, that connects the notes A and G. Start the first note using tonguing, but let the air continue without stopping as you move smoothly between the two notes that are connected with the slur.

Vocabulary

In medieval times, musicians and other entertainers were called **minstrels**. Traveling minstrels were common, going from place to place to entertain. (See *Jolly Minstrels*, p.19)

6/8 time

6/8 time means there are 6 beats in every bar and an eighth note (ti) is counted as one beat. The music will have a rocking feel to it. Beat one and beat four will be stronger sounds or pulses in the music. The sample below is from *Jolly Minstrels* (p.19). There is also a one-beat anacrusis at the beginning of the song. (See a more detailed explanation of anacrusis on p.13)

Tied notes

A tie is a line that connects two notes that are <u>the same pitch</u>. The value of both notes are added together to create one longer sound. The tie in bar 4 of *Jolly Minstrels* means that you play the low E and hold it for 5 counts (3 + 2). (see sample above)

Dotted eighth note

A dot placed after a note increases the note's duration by one half. All notes can be dotted. *Day is Done* (p.19) has an eighth note with a dot. The dotted note has borrowed some of the value of the next eighth note so all that is left over is a sixteenth note (or the last part of a tiki-tiki) which is quite short. This two-note combination has a lilting feel and it is read as "tim-ki" when using Kodaly rhythm duration syllables.

(Sample: *Day is Done, p.19*)

Day is Done also has a dotted half note. The time value of the half note is two beats. The dot adds half of that (2 + 1) to create a three-beat note. You will see another dotted note (a dotted quarter note) in the Blue Knight song challenge, *Ode to Joy* (p.21).

Rit.

Rit. is an abbreviation of an Italian word that means gradually slowing down. It is often used at the end of a song. See *Lady of the Red Castle* (p.18) and *Day is Done* (p.19).

Fermata

The fermata symbol (also called a pause)   placed over a note, means the note is to be held longer than the value written. A fermata is written at the end of *Day is Done* (p.19). If you are playing with the accompaniment track, just let the note fade away.

Finger push-ups

Practice finger push-ups to help you improve your transitions to high D. Most of the fingerings involve moving between B and D'. Practice ten B-D' push-ups to prepare before playing.

Lady of the Red Castle

À la claire fontaine

Royal Recorders Copyright © 2022 Donna Rhodenizer / Red Castle Publishing
www.royalrecorders.com

Jolly Minstrels

Day is Done

7 - *BLUE KNIGHT* in Training

New note: High C (C')

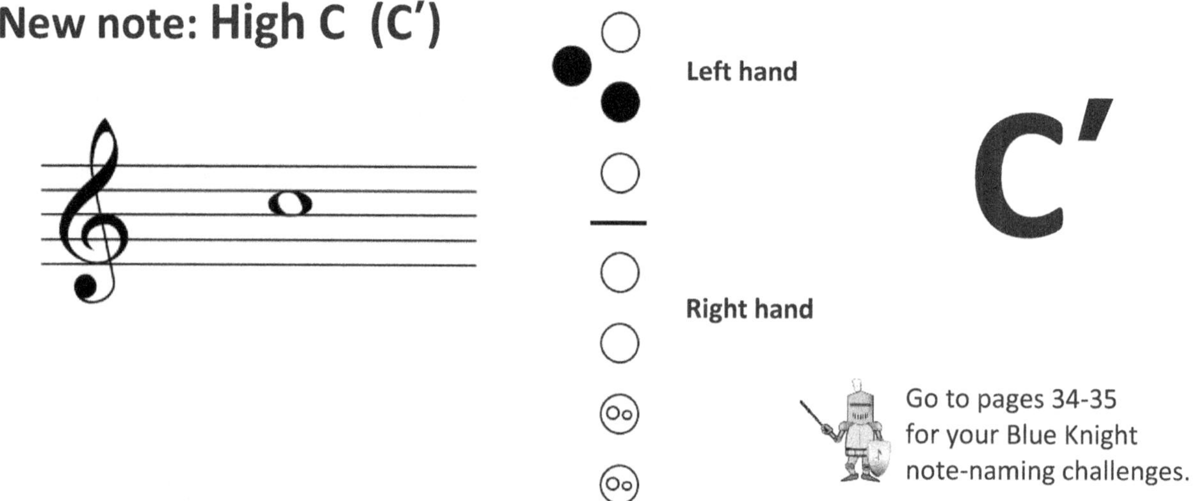

Dotted quarter note

In the song *Ode to Joy* (p.21) there is a dotted quarter note and an eighth note combination. Together, they add up to two beats. The quarter note gets one full beat plus half of its value. The extra half beat is borrowed from the next note, leaving only half a beat, or an eighth note. When reading with Kodaly rhythm duration syllables we say tam ti for this combination.

(Sample: *Ode to Joy*)

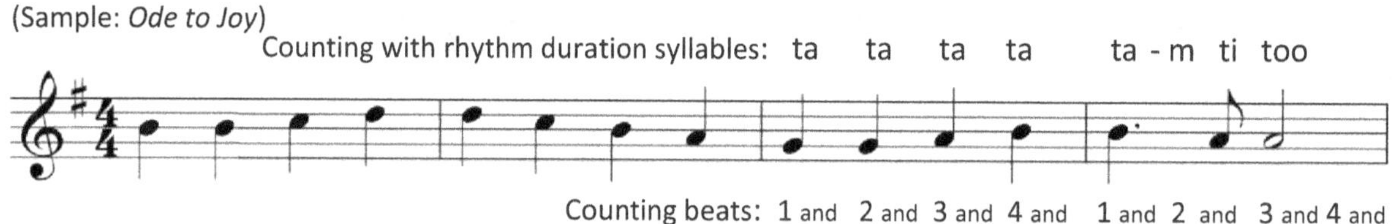

When counting beats, say "and" between each of the beats, counting "1 and 2 and 3 and 4 and". This doesn't change the number of beats (there are still only 4 beats in the bar) but it makes it easier to see how the dotted-note rhythm fits within the four beats of the bar.

Similar phrases / practice tip

The first three bars of *Ode to Joy* are repeated to create the first three bars of phrase two and phrase four. Beethoven only makes slight changes in the last bar of each of these phrases to make them different. Because you play the same note combinations in these phrases three times, they are going to improve quickly. The third phrase (bars 9-12) is the most difficult line of the song and it only shows up once. **Practice tip**: when you are practicing, start with the third phrase. Play it slowly several times before you play the whole song. When you finally put the song together, the third line will be ready and well prepared!

Rests

Pay attention to the rests in *Oh When the Saints* (p.22). There is no rest in the opening bar, but it only has 3 beats (starting on beat 2) and it is acting like a "3-beat anacrusis". You will find the "missing beat one" at the end of the song. At the beginning of bars 3, 5, 9 do not hold the notes into the quarter rests. These are good spots to take a breath. Also, the half rest at the beginning of bar 13 lasts for two beats. It is important to count and play accurately, including the parts of the music that involve NO sound!

Royal Recorders Copyright © 2022 Donna Rhodenizer / Red Castle Publishing
www.royalrecorders.com

Cabbage Soup

Ode to Joy
(From the Ninth Symphony)

Royal Recorders Copyright © 2022 Donna Rhodenizer / Red Castle Publishing
www.royalrecorders.com

7 - *BLUE KNIGHT* Song Challenges

Oh When the Saints

Traditional

My Composition: ____

____
Composer

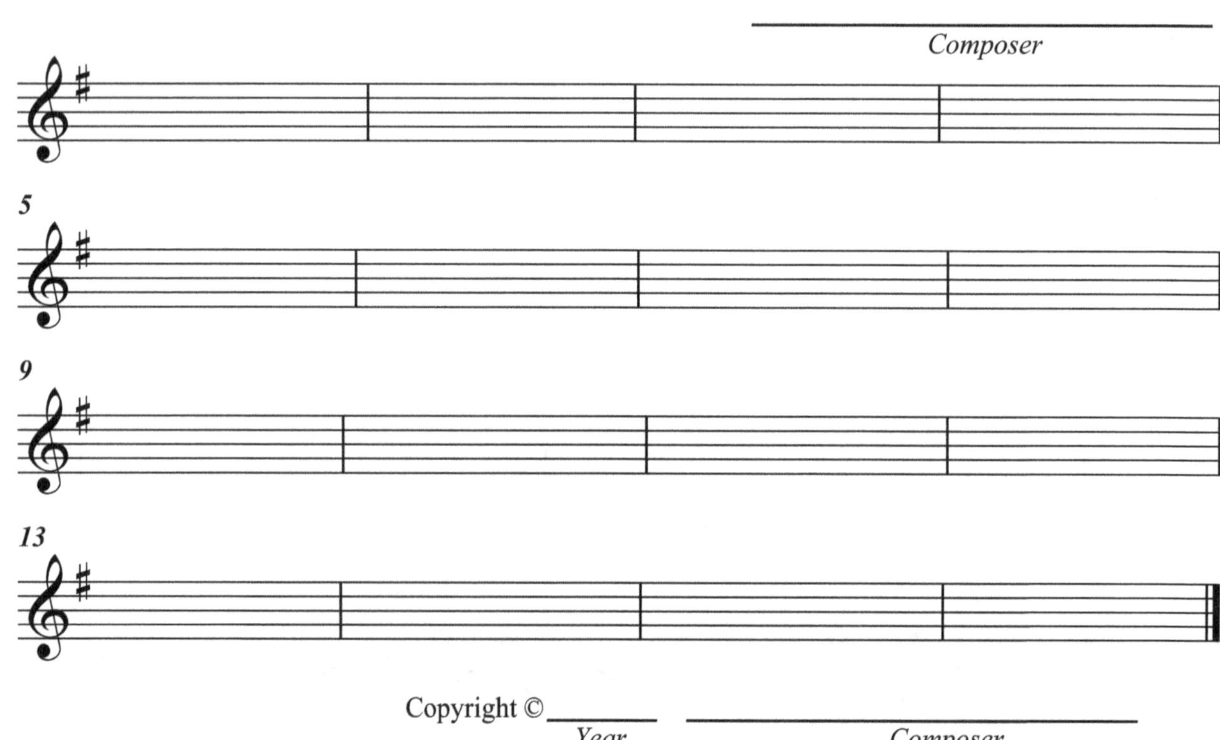

Copyright ©________ ________________________________
Year   *Composer*

Royal Recorders Copyright © 2022 Donna Rhodenizer / Red Castle Publishing
www.royalrecorders.com

Royal Recorders

Knightly Note-naming Challenges

You will need a timer

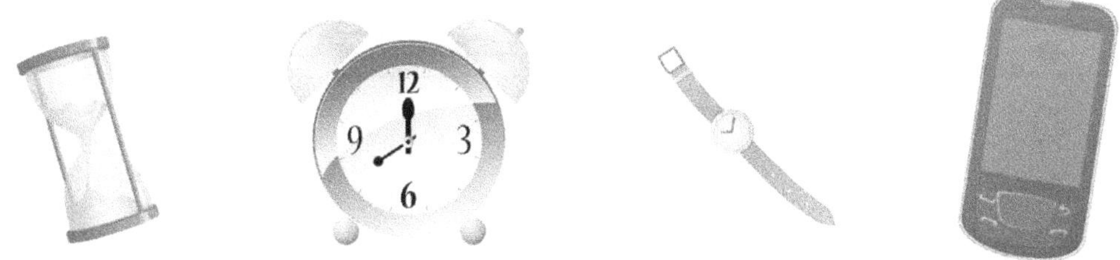

Set the timer for 2 minutes.
Name as many notes as you can in two minutes.
There are 30-note Challenges and 60-note Challenges.
OR
See how long it takes you to name all 30 or 60 notes.
Keep track of your best time!

**If you can do the 60-note Challenge
in ONE minute
you are naming one note EVERY second!**

For more note-naming sheets go to **www.royalrecorders.com**

WHITE, YELLOW, ORANGE Knights
30-note Challenges

Introducing G A B

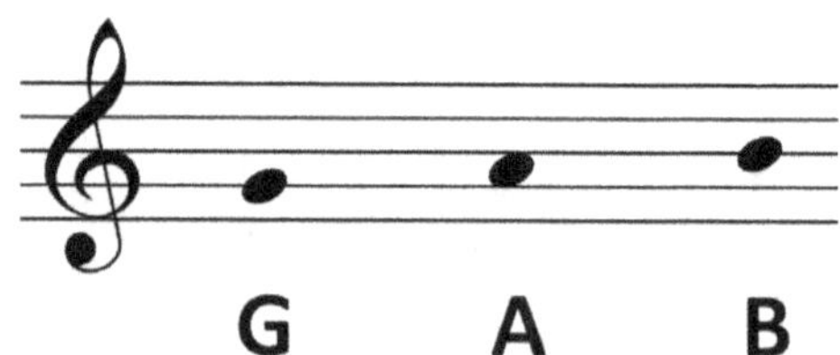

Name these **G A B** notes

15

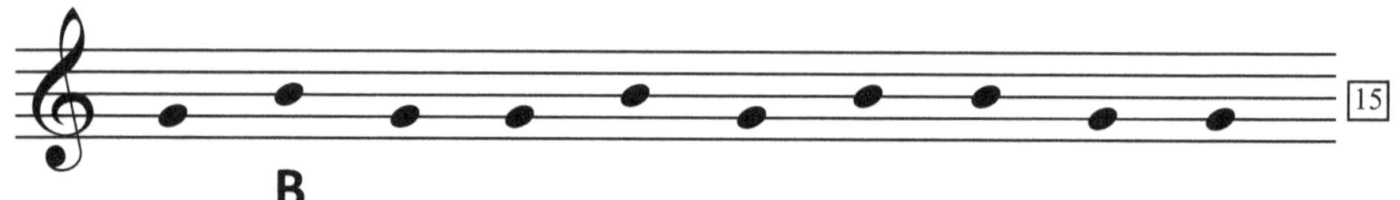

15

15

/30

Name these **G A B** notes 

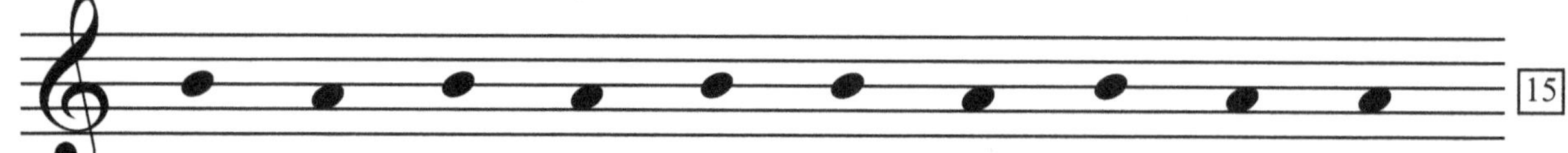

15

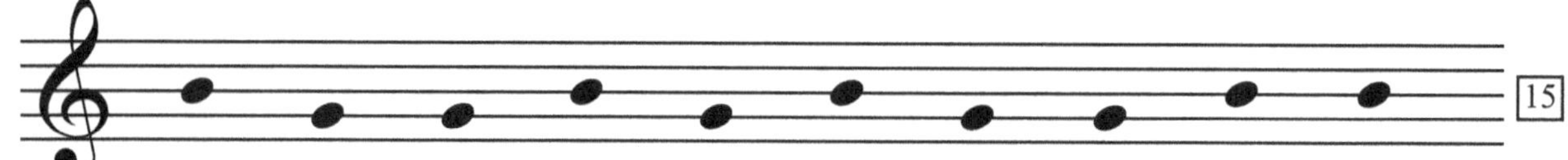

15

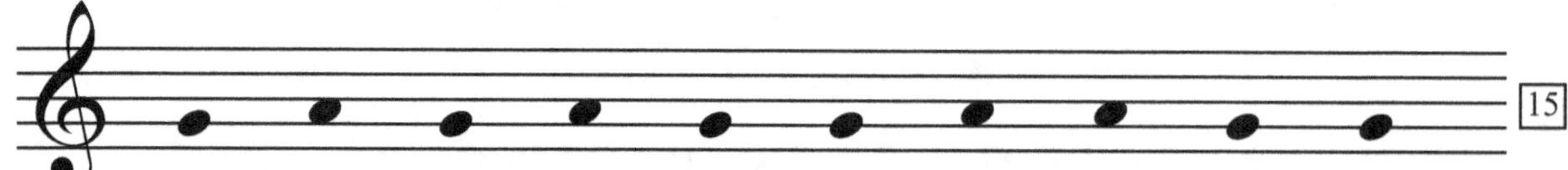

15

/30

WHITE, YELLOW, ORANGE Knights
30-note Challenges

Name these **G A B** notes

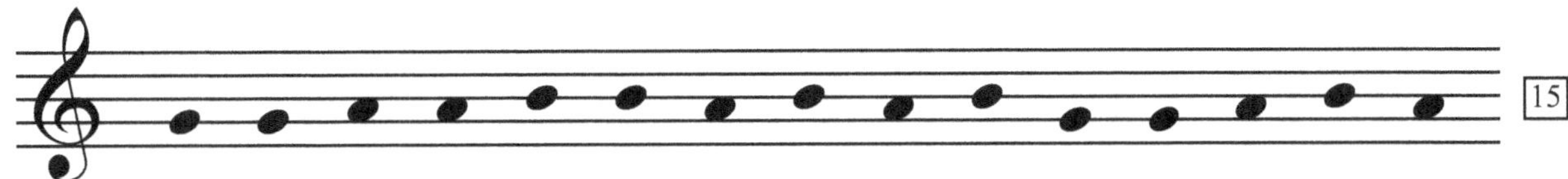

Name these **G A B** notes

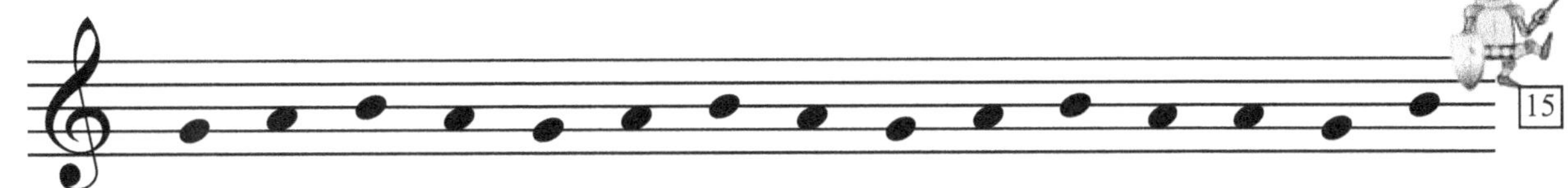

Name these **G A B** notes

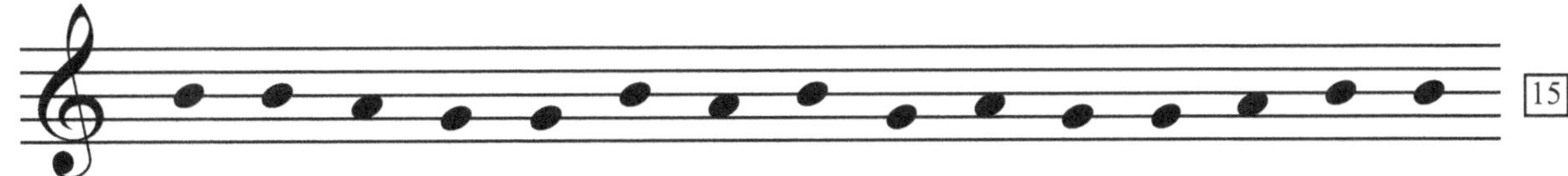

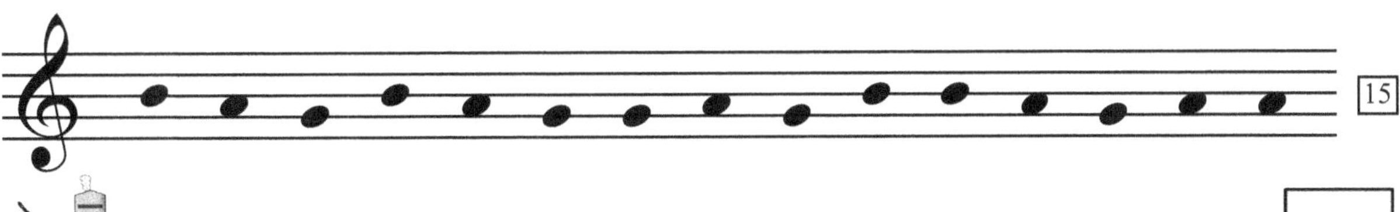

WHITE, YELLOW, ORANGE Knights
60-note Challenges

WHITE, YELLOW, ORANGE Knights

60-note Challenges

Name these **G A B** notes

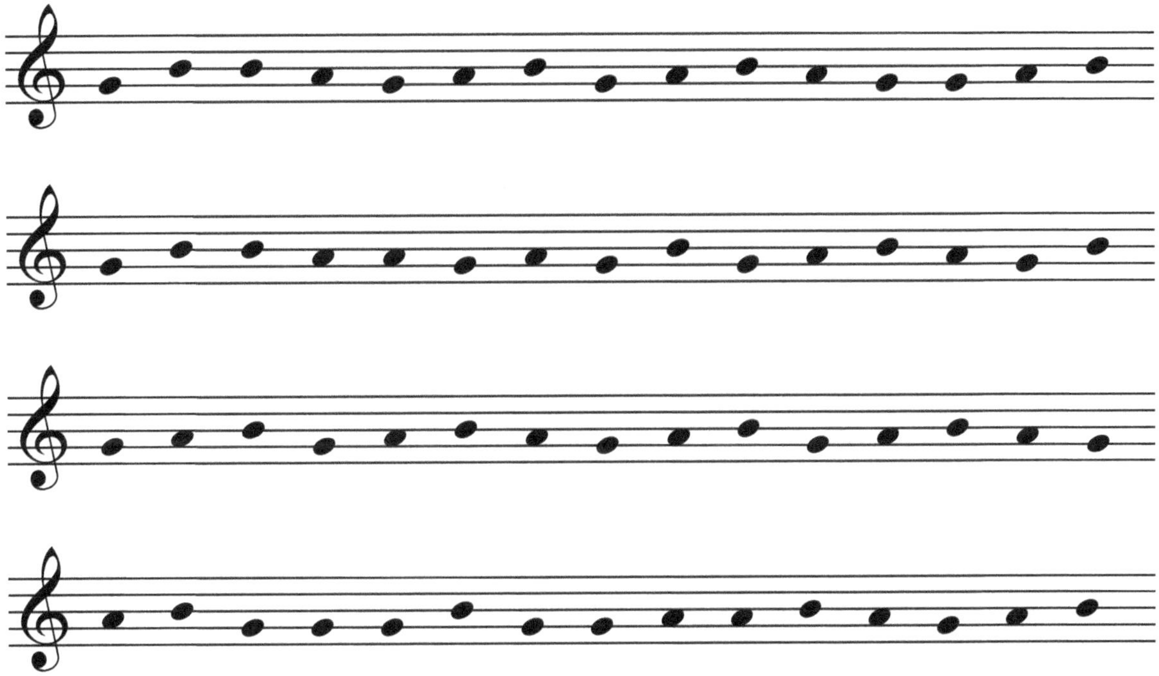

15

15

15

15

/60

Name these **G A B** notes

15

15

15

15

/60

Royal Recorders Copyright © 2022 Donna Rhodenizer / Red Castle Publishing
www.royalrecorders.com

GREEN KNIGHT
30-note Challenges

Introducing E

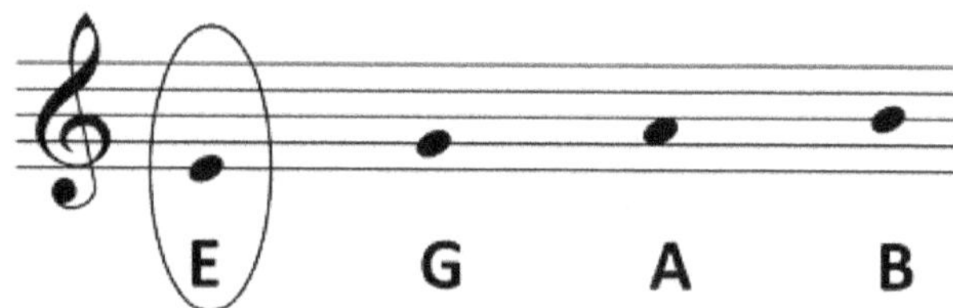

Name these **E G A B** notes

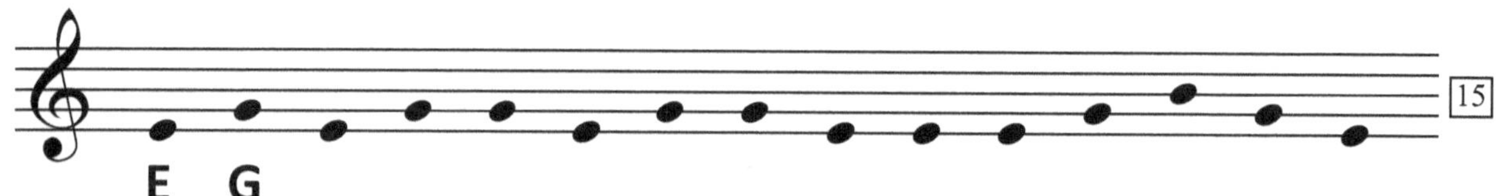

Name these **E G A B** notes

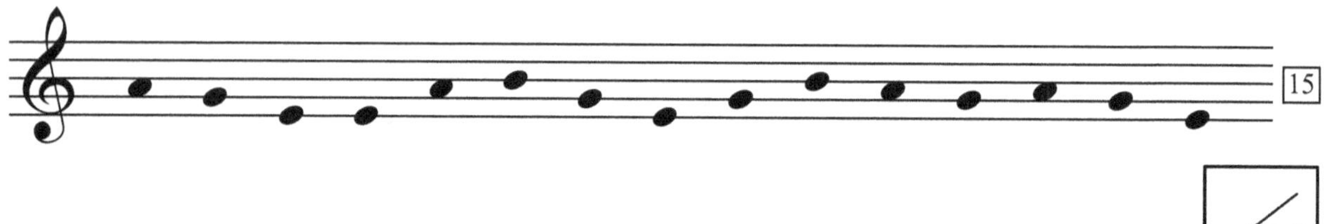

Name these **E G A B** notes

GREEN KNIGHT
60-note Challenges

Name these **E G A B** notes

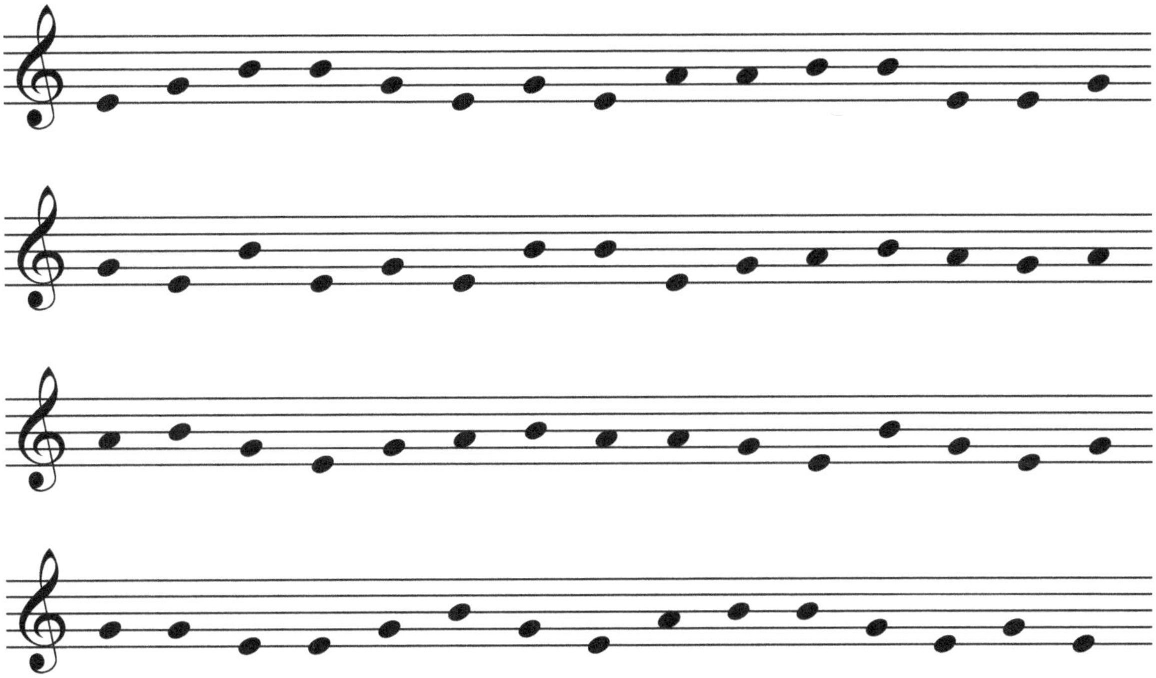

15

15

15

15

/60

Name these **E G A B** notes

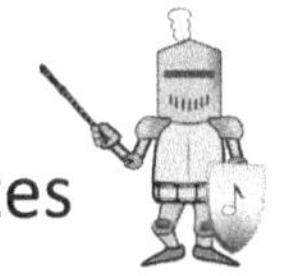

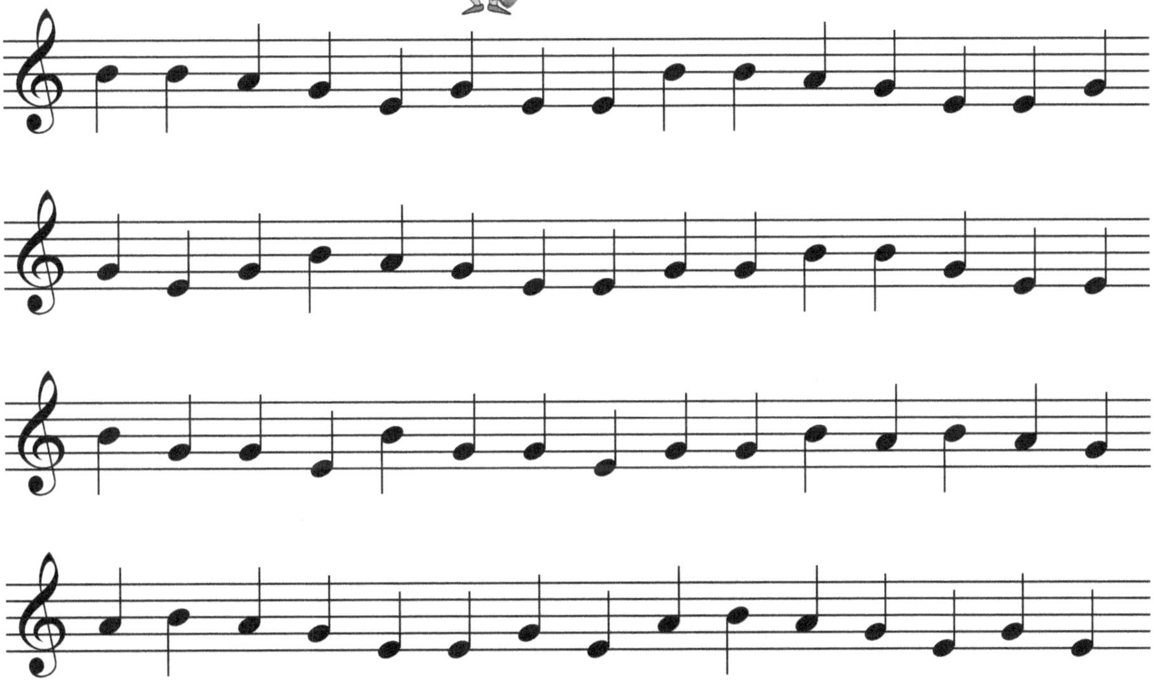

15

15

15

15

/60

PURPLE KNIGHT
30-note Challenges

Introducing Low D

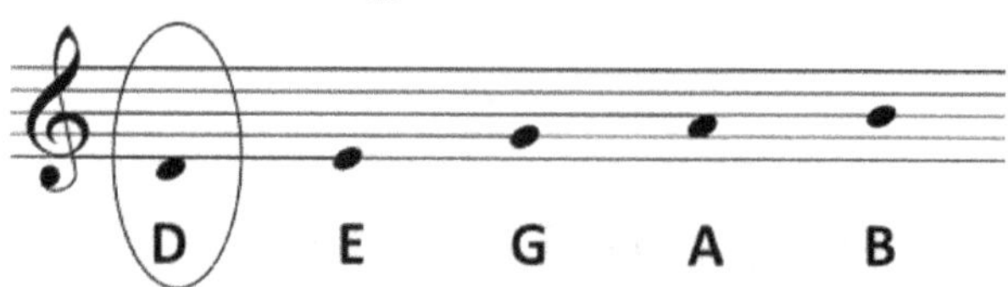

Name these **D E G A B** notes

D E   G A B

Name these **D E G A B** notes

Name these **D E G A B** notes

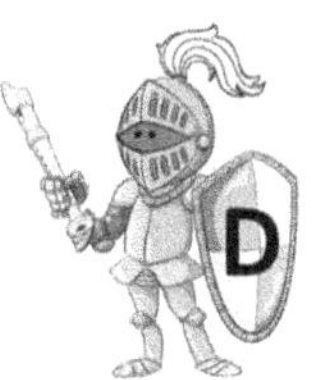

PURPLE KNIGHT

60-note Challenges

Name these **D E G A B** notes

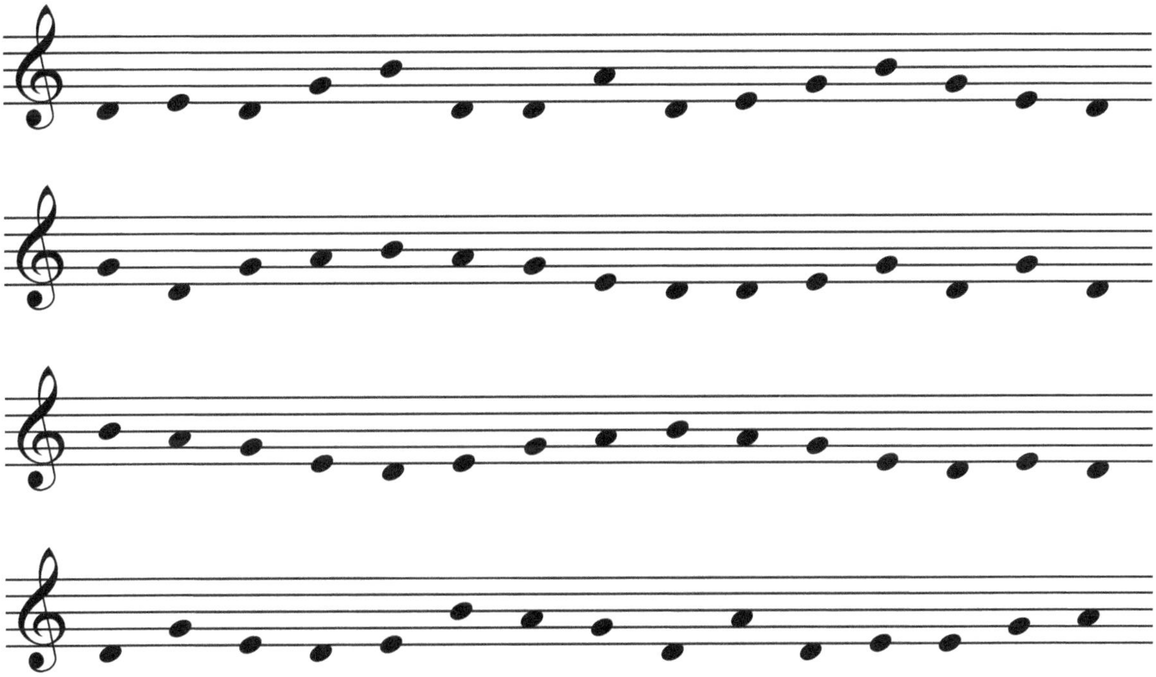

15

15

15

15

/60

Name these **D E G A B** notes

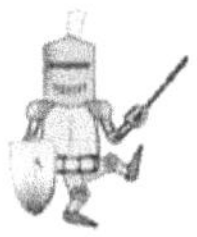

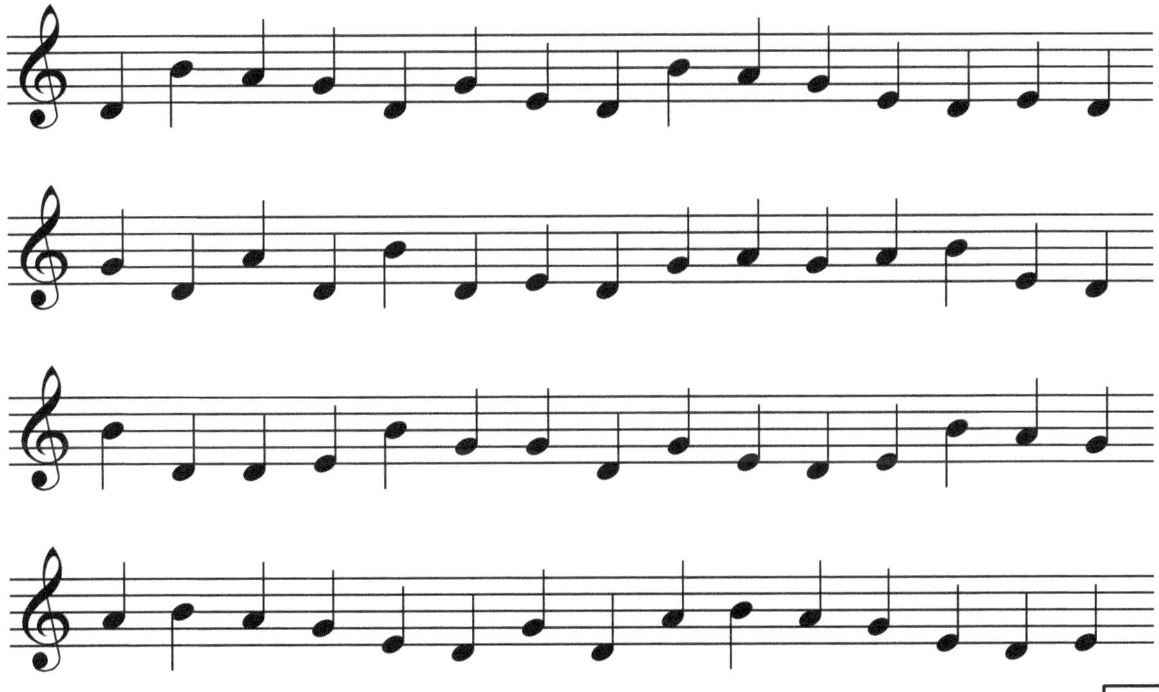

15

15

15

15

/60

Royal Recorders Copyright © 2022 Donna Rhodenizer / Red Castle Publishing
www.royalrecorders.com

TURQUOISE KNIGHT
30-note Challenges

Introducing D'

Name these **D E G A B D'** notes

D' **D**

Name these **D E G A B D'** notes

Name these **D E G A B D'** notes

TURQUOISE KNIGHT
60-note Challenges

Name these **D E G A B D'** notes

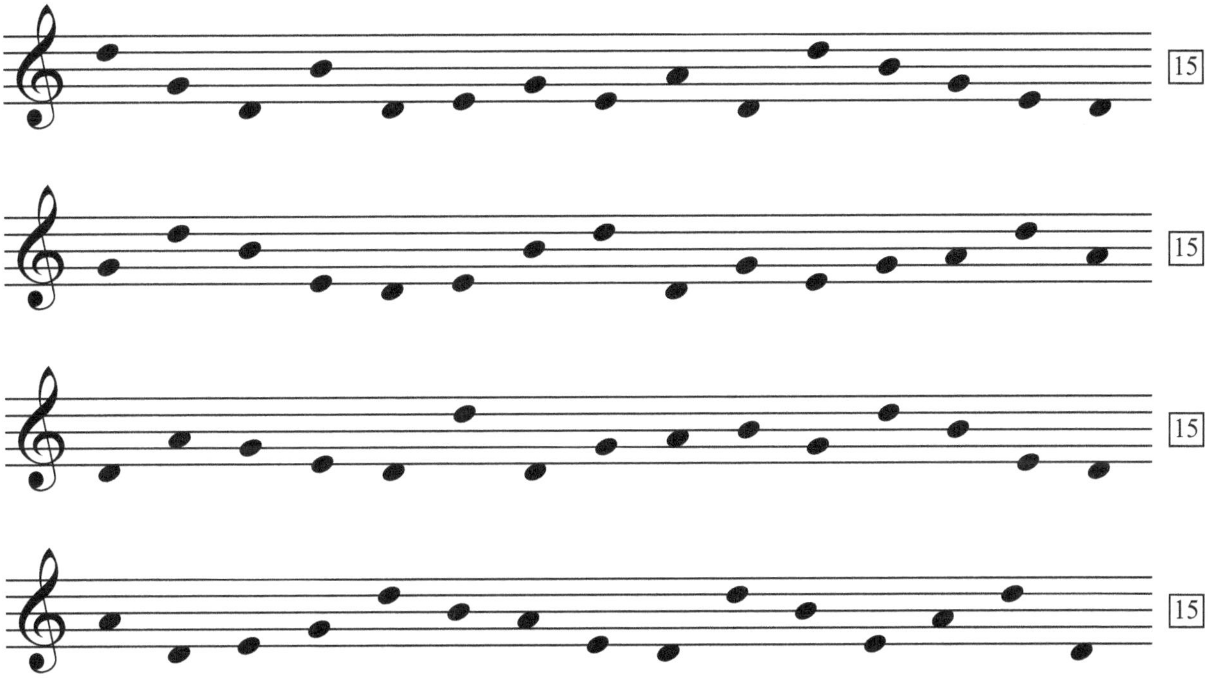

Name these **D E G A B D'** notes

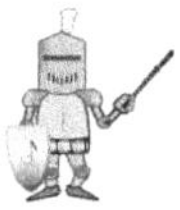

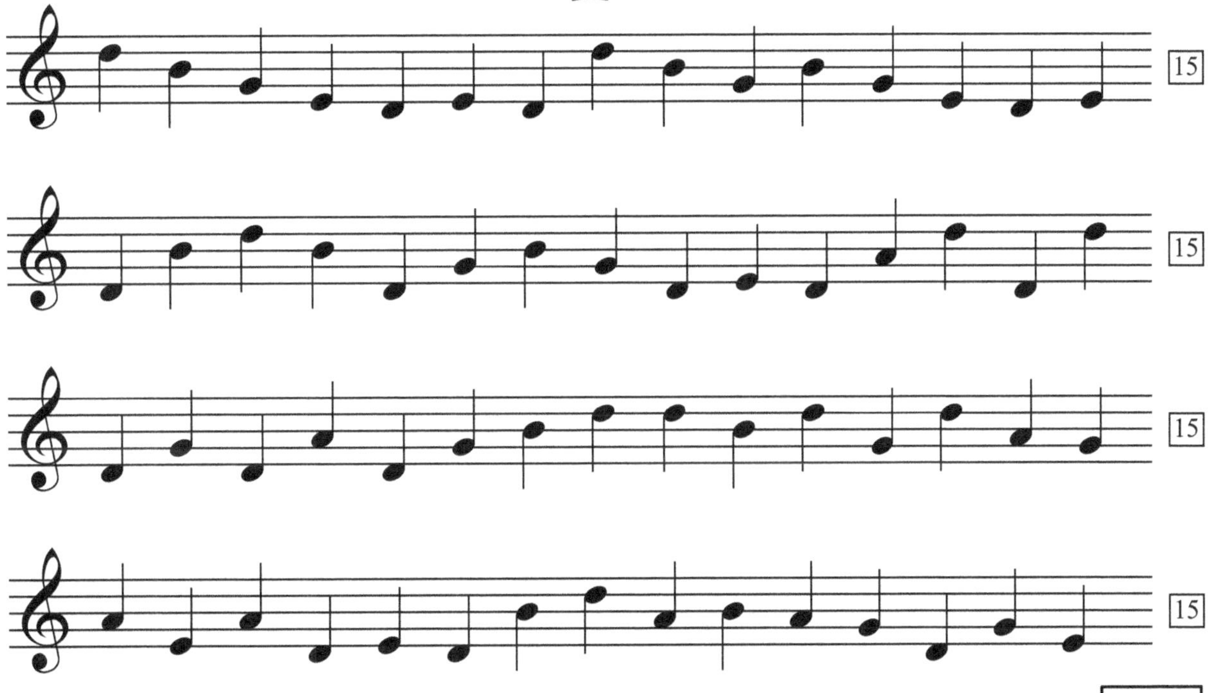

BLUE KNIGHT
30-note Challenges

Introducing C'

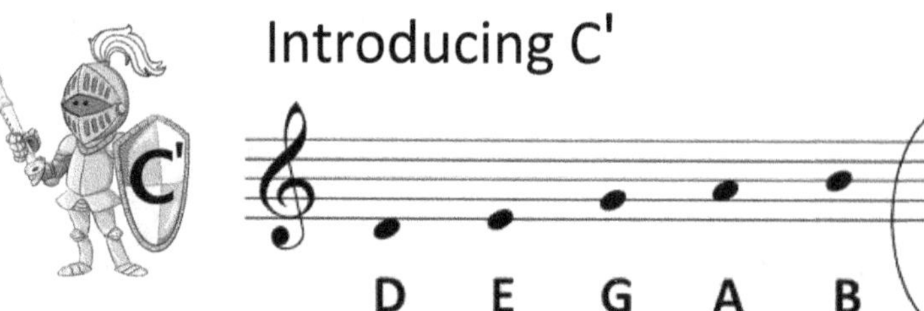

Name these **D E G A B C' D'** notes

Name these **D E G A B C' D'** notes

Royal Recorders Copyright © 2022 Donna Rhodenizer / Red Castle Publishing
www.royalrecorders.com

BLUE KNIGHT
60-note Challenges

Name these **D E G A B C' D'** notes

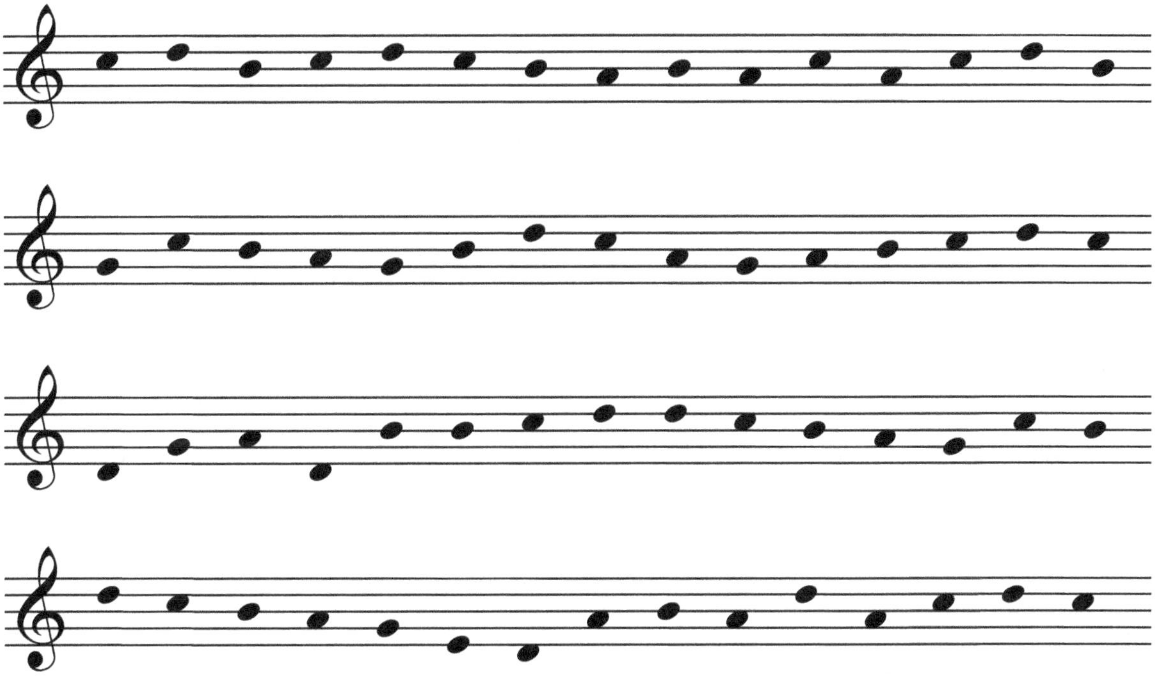

15

15

15

15

/60

Name these **D E G A B C' D'** notes

15

15

15

15

/60

Royal Recorders Copyright © 2022 Donna Rhodenizer / Red Castle Publishing
www.royalrecorders.com

Royal Recorders

BOOK 1 notes:
(in order of introduction)

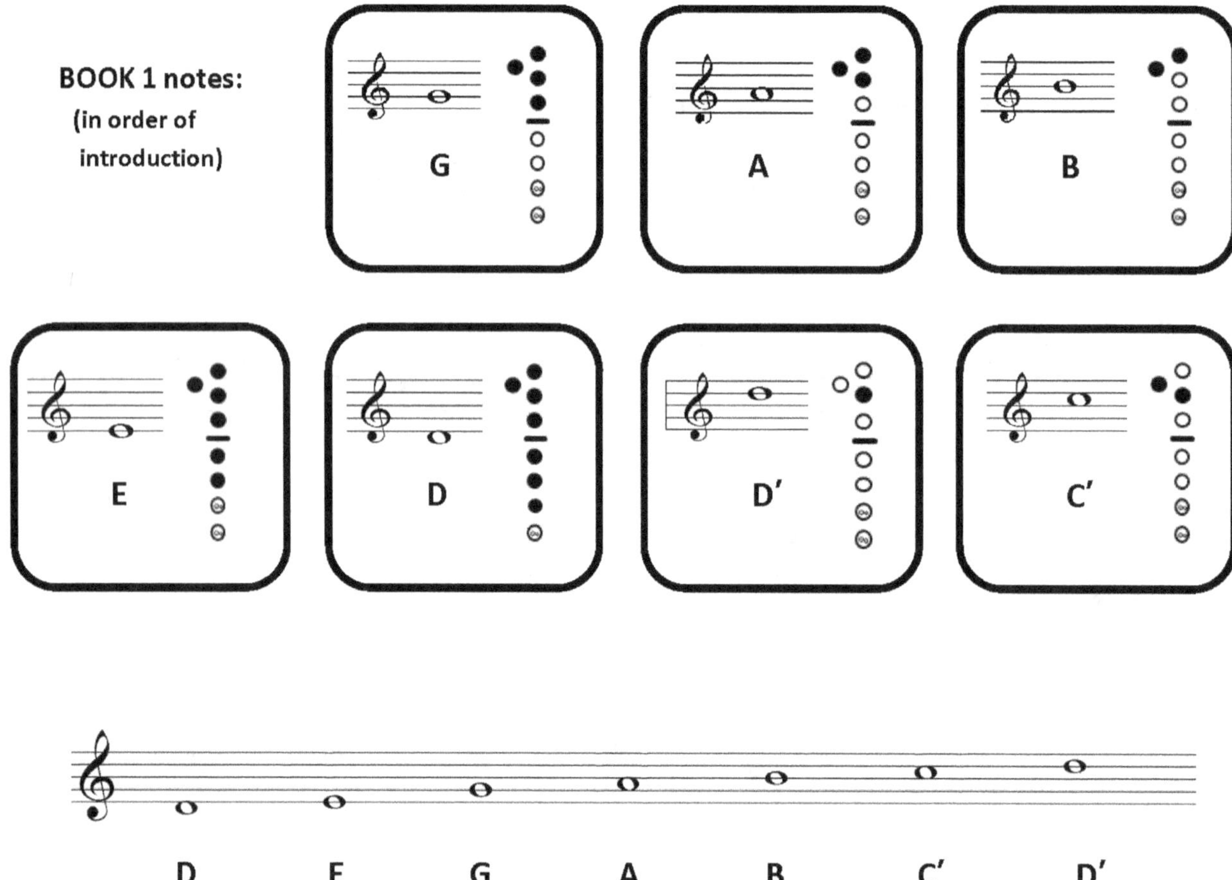

Printable copy of *Royal Recorders* fingering charts are available at www.royalrecorders.com
Printable fingering charts for the entire range of notes for Descant to Sub-contra-bass recorders
are available from Dolmetsch (online) with permission granted to make copies:
Baroque/English Recorder Fingering Chart https://www.dolmetsch.com/efingeringchart.pdf
German Recorder Fingering Chart - https://www.dolmetsch.com/gfingeringchart.pdf

Visit www.royalrecorders.com for:

- MP3 accompaniments for all songs (in practice and performance speeds)
- Track information for all accompaniments
- Additional note-naming sheets
- More songs!

Royal Recorders Copyright © 2022 Donna Rhodenizer / Red Castle Publishing
www.royalrecorders.com

ROYAL RECORDERS

BOOK 1

CERTIFICATE
OF COMPLETION

This certificate is proudly presented to

Knight in Training

Music teacher

Date

Royal Recorders Copyright © 2022 Donna Rhodenizer / Red Castle Publishing
www.royalrecorders.com

www.ingramcontent.com/pod-product-compliance
Lightning Source LLC
Chambersburg PA
CBHW080334030726
47593CB00010B/3004